FUN WITH PATTERN

D1441999

BY FIFI WEINERT

THE METROPOLITAN MUSEUM OF ART
VIKING

NEW YORK

VIKING

First published in 1995 by The Metropolitan Museum of Art, New York, and Viking,
a division of Penguin Books USA Inc., 375 Hudson Street, New York, New York 10014,
and Penguin Books Canada Ltd., 10 Alcorn Avenue, Toronto, Ontario, Canada M4V 3B2

10 9 8 7 6 5 4 3 2

ISBN 0-87099-747-5 MMA
ISBN 0-670-86323-8 Viking

Produced by the Department of Special Publications,
The Metropolitan Museum of Art
Manager, Robie Rogge
Editor, Mary Beth Brewer
Production, Cathy Hansen

Stamp illustrations by Larry Boyer
Activity illustrations by Robin Rule
Page composition by Sophia Stavropoulos
Design by Miriam Berman
Printed in China

CONTENTS

INTRODUCTION

Pattern surrounds us, both in the natural world and in the world that we have created. It is so common that we barely notice it. Go on a pattern hunt in your own house. How many patterns can you find? Start inside with tiles, wallpaper designs, and even the burners on top of your stove. Look outside at the posts of a picket fence or the windows of your building. You will quickly see that we live in a patterned world.

Why is there so much pattern? Because pattern is comforting. It is organized, predictably repetitive. Yet it can be surprisingly filled with whimsy, energy, and complexity. It is also fun to make.

Pattern decorates all sorts of surfaces. It is made of paper, wood, sand, stone, leather, fibers, clay, plastic, metal, and glass. It is woven, chiseled, carved, welded, embroidered, molded, pierced, pieced, stenciled, painted, printed, dyed, and photographed onto and into the surfaces it decorates. The first step in becoming an expert in making pattern is noticing pattern when you see it.

What is pattern? Simply stated it is the orderly repetition of an image or images. The images repeated in pattern are called motifs. Any image can serve as a motif. The stamps included in this kit feature twenty-four motifs.

Among the motifs in this kit are a circle, a triangle, a flower, and a leaf.

Although beautiful designs can be created by arranging motifs randomly, these designs are not patterns. To be a pattern, a design must be based on regular repetition of one or more motifs.

Humans have always decorated the objects they make with pattern. An amazing wealth of ornament is found throughout the world, from all cultures and times. The following pages contain examples of many ways pattern has been used throughout history. Some of the patterns you will see have been interpreted with the stamps in this kit.

In this mosaic from ancient Rome, a water goddess rides a sea horse. She is surrounded by a design composed of bold triangles, chevrons and ropes.

8

Half circles and geometric shapes ornament this plate made during the Renaissance in Italy.

A silver figure of a kneeling bull, from ancient Iran, bears repeating bands of ornamentation.

9

This jacket from nineteenth-century China is patterned with small diamond-shaped pieces of silk that have been sewn together.

An ancient Near Eastern crafts-person hammered concentric circles into this golden ewer in about 2100 B.C.

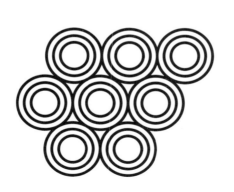

A painter named Euphronios signed this Greek vase in about 515 B.C. Showing young Athenians arming for a battle, it is decorated with bands of palmettes.

11

In Renaissance Italy, artists created this scene from tiny bits of wood. It decorated the study of an Italian duke and features fields of triangles, bands of braid, and a wealth of other patterns.

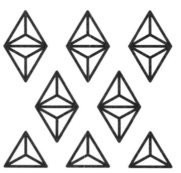

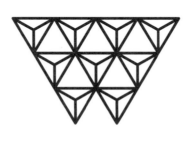

Spirals make up the head and body of this gold and ivory frog pendant crafted in Panama between 1200 and 1400.

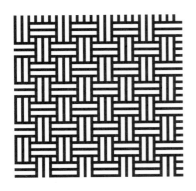

In Nigeria in the sixteenth century, artists in the court of Benin adorned shrines with bronze heads of their rulers. On this one, the cap, hair, and collar are all richly decorated with pattern.

14

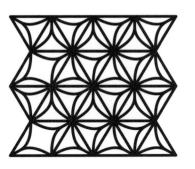

This courtyard was built for a private home in Damascus, Syria, in 1707. It shows a dazzling array of patterns, many composed of triangles.

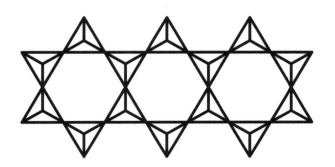

15

Pattern is often used in borders. Here, on a parade shield designed for King Louis XIV of France in about 1700, the ferocious head of Medusa is surrounded by a border of braid.

This ceramic vessel was created in southwest Iran in about 2900 B.C. The artist created a lively pattern of parallel lines to represent the boar's rough bristles.

USING THE STAMPS

Each of the twenty-four stamps in this kit contains an image, or motif. These motifs can be combined to form an infinite number of patterns. The chart inside the cover suggests some ways you can combine the stamp images. Here are some other possibilities.

Eleven of the stamp images interconnect with themselves and each other. These are especially versatile in creating complex motifs and running patterns.

Two of the motifs can make patterns longer or larger.

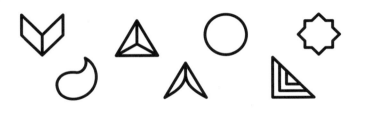

Seven of the motifs are basic geometric or organic shapes. They can be used in countless ways.

Some of the patterns they make require overlapping stamp imprints.

Leaves and flowers appear on three stamps.

And there are three classical images, the palmette, the spiral, and the fret.

These motifs were quite popular in ancient Greece, where they often appeared in pattern rows or bands.

Finally, some motifs can nest inside others or inside larger shapes made by joining several stamp imprints together.

Which stamps were used to make these shapes?

(The answer is on page 73.)

MAKE A GIFT BOX

You will need a washed milk or juice carton, a pair of scissors, a ruler, paper, tape, and glue or rubber cement.

1. Open the top of the carton. Put a piece of tape around all four sides of the carton three inches from its bottom.

2. Cut two of the carton's corners down to the tape line, freeing one side. Fold that side back. It will become your box lid.

3. Cut off the three remaining sides along the top of the tape line. Turn the box around. Fold the lid over the top.

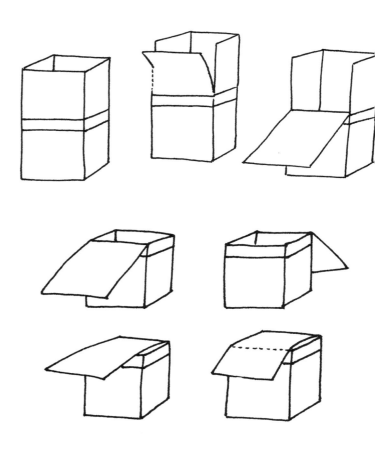

22

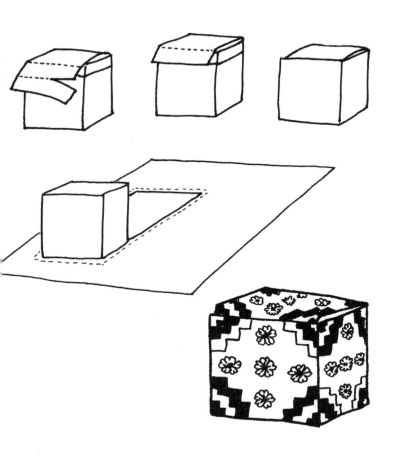

4. Continue folding the lid down the front of the carton so that it forms a long tab.

5. Trim the tab to one inch.

6. Fold the tab inside the box. Remove the tape.

7. To decorate the box, open the lid and lay the box flat on a sheet of paper. Trace. Next trace each of the other sides. Stamp out a design on each of your tracings. Color them. Cut them out and glue them to the box. Trim off any excess paper.

CREATING PATTERN BANDS

Pattern is based on the simple idea that repetition is exciting.

Motifs, or images, are repeated in pattern. You begin creating pattern by choosing a motif. Then you must decide how you want to repeat it. Here are some of the ways one motif can be repeated in one row, or band, of pattern.

A motif can be printed in one direction.

Or in alternating directions.

Or it can be rotated on the diagonal.

Small or large spaces can be placed between motifs.

Several motifs can be combined in one row.

And a row can be printed vertically.

25

You can vary the sequence of motifs and the sequence of motifs and spaces. Just remember that if you create a complicated sequence you must repeat the entire sequence to make a pattern.

How would you continue these patterns?

(The answer is on page 73.)

PLAYING WITH PATTERN

You can use line to make your pattern more whimsical or more decorative. Line can finish off awkward edges in a pattern or it can join parts of a pattern that don't exactly mesh.

One design appears at the top of this page. Three ways of changing it with line (and, in the center, with one other stamp) appear below it.

(To see how it's done, turn to page 74.)

27

A photocopier can change the size of the patterns you stamp out. Small-scale patterns look dainty. Large-scale patterns look bold. Enlarging pattern creates empty spaces you can decorate with line or other motifs.

Color establishes the mood of a pattern. Color makes a pattern cheerful or somber, calm or lively. How many ways can you color this pattern band? (Stamp it out, and then color it in.)

MAKE A PICTURE FRAME

You will need a business-size envelope, a pair of scissors, and crayons, markers, or colored pencils.

1. Seal an envelope, then fold it in half.

2. Trim off the two short edges.

3. Unfold the envelope. Stamp any pattern on the sealed side, then color it. (This will be the back of your picture frame.) Turn the envelope over and print a border design on each half of the envelope's front. (Suggested patterns appear on the opposite page.)

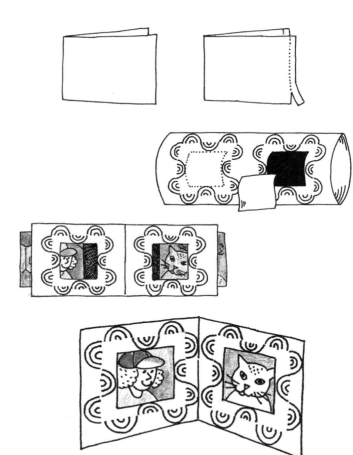

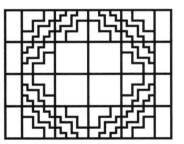

The dotted lines show where you will need to complete the pattern with a pencil, crayon, or marker.

4. Carefully pull the front and back of your envelope apart, then cut out a square or rectangle inside each of the border designs. Be careful not to cut through the back of the envelope! Now color your frame.

5. Slide a picture into each side, then sharply fold the envelope so it will stand securely.

JOINING PATTERN BANDS

Rows of pattern are called pattern bands. Bands can be horizontal, vertical, diagonal, or curved. Many large areas of pattern are made by joining pattern bands side by side. Both of these patterns are built with rows of design that have been joined together.

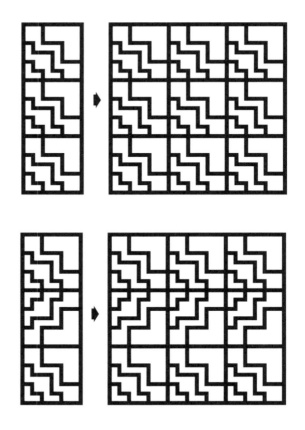

nds can be joined together
thout changing their direction.

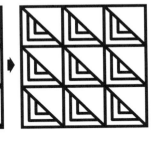

Alternate rows of
pattern can be flipped.

Pattern bands can
be repeated in all
the ways you
repeat a motif.

ws can be printed
uching each other.

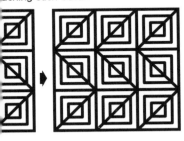

And rows can be printed with
spaces between them.

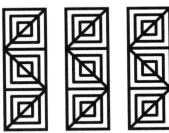

You can combine different rows of pattern.

You can alternate motifs within rows.

And you can vary the sequence in which different rows of pattern are printed. But once you set the rules of your pattern you must follow those rules throughout your design.

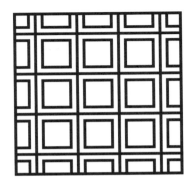

Of course, you can play with allover patterns using line, color, or scale. The pattern at the top of the page has been turned into a stripe and a diagonal stripe. Now try turning it into a checked pattern.

(The answer is on page 74.)

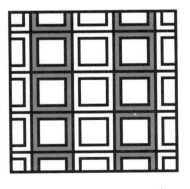

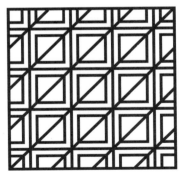

35

MAKE A CHECKERBOARD AND CHECKERS

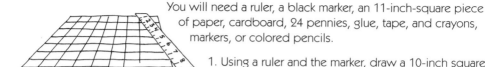

You will need a ruler, a black marker, an 11-inch-square piece of paper, cardboard, 24 pennies, glue, tape, and crayons, markers, or colored pencils.

1. Using a ruler and the marker, draw a 10-inch square on the paper. Divide the square into 10 rows of one-inch squares.

2. Stamp out the checkerboard following the diagram on the right.

3. Color the palmettes one color and the frets another, then color the border in contrasting colors.

4. Cut out the board. To make it sturdier, glue it to a piece of cardboard. If you like, decorate the back of the board with a pattern.

5. Now make your checkers. Using the half circle stamp, print 24 circles.

Color 12 circles in one color and 12 in another, then cut them out. Tape a penny to the back of each checker to give them weight.

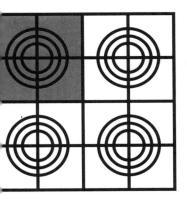

PATTERN TILES

These designs could be built with bands of pattern. But it is easier to build them by joining pattern tiles together. A tile is a square or rectangular block of design. All of these patterns were made by repeating a pattern tile. The tile that is repeated in the first three of the patterns is shown in gray. Can you find the tile that is repeated in the fourth design?

(The answer is on page 74.)

Larger tiles give you room for more complicated designs. This means more surprises can occur when you join your tiles together.

You can join tiles together in wide bands of pattern, just the way you join smaller motifs into bands. Then you can turn your bands into large allover designs. Tile patterns are perfect for wrapping paper. Use the grid on page 58 to help you make large patterns. Make a photocopy of the grid, then print your tile on it. Use your stamped out tile as a guide. Place it under the paper you are printing on. It will help you remember how you made your tile.

PATTERN PUZZLES

ISLAMIC PLATES

Iznik is a city in northwestern Turkey. From about 1400 until 1700, it was famous for its brilliant ceramic pottery and tiles. Spirals and flowers like the ones seen on the plate at the right often decorate the ware, but the motifs are never combined in exactly the same way.

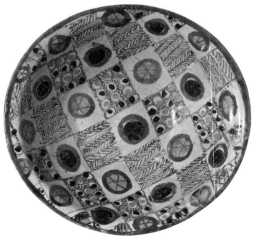

The bowl on the left was made in Iraq in the ninth century out of glazed clay decorated with patterns in metallic paint, called luster.

Try stamping out the patterns seen on both plates.

(To see how it's done, turn to page 75.)

MODEL OF A SERVANT

This wooden model of a servant comes from ancient Egypt. It was found in the tomb of a man named Mekutra, who died about four thousand years ago in the city of Thebes. The woman carries provisions for her master—in one hand she holds a duck, and the basket on her head is filled with bread, vegetables, and meat.

Using these three stamps, try to stamp out the patterns that decorate her dress.

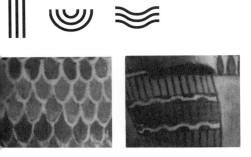

(See how it's done on page 76.)

NECK-AMPHORA

Two views of a terracotta storage vessel, known as an amphora, are shown on the left. It was made in Greece in the seventh century bc. It shows the hero Heracles slaying the centaur Nessos. Surrounding the scene are many lovely patterns. Can you stamp out four of them?

(Some possibilities can be found on page 76.)

EGYPTIAN PATTERNS

These delightfully varied patterns come from the ceiling of an Egyptian tomb. Try stamping them out, then use them to decorate note cards or wrapping paper.

(Turn to page 77 for ways of recreating the designs.)

43

CRIB QUILT

This quilt was made in Pennsylvania about one hundred and fifty years ago for a baby's crib. It i hand-stitched in rec calico and plain white cloth. There is more than one way to stamp out the central pattern. Can you figure out one way using this stamp?

Can you also make the pattern using the circle stamp and a ruler?

There are also two ways to create the border pattern using different stamps.

(Turn to page 77 to see the solutions.)

Can you copy the "S" shape in its design using this stamp?

PERUVIAN TUNIC

This tunic was made of wool and cotton in the seventh to eighth century.

(The answer is on page 78.)

45

MEDIEVAL PLAQUE

This ornamental copper plaque, made about 1200 in Germany, is decorated in a pattern of colored enamel and gold.

ITALIAN ALBARELLO (MEDICINE JAR)

The motif that decorates this Italian jar is very similar to the one found on the medieval plaque. It consists of a diamond with semicircles on its sides. How many different ways can you recreate the pattern?

And how many different motifs can you invent to nest inside the diamond? Decorate the designs you create with markers. (Some suggestions are on page 78.)

ANIAN PRAYER
CHE

eautiful, intricate
atterns decorate
e surfaces of many
amic works of art.
is niche was
ade in about 1354
om tiny pieces of
ed ceramic.
sing three stamps,
v to create this
attern:

ere's how
begins:

urn to page 78 to see
ow it continues.)

MAKE A BOOK JACKET

You will need a large sheet of paper, tape, a ruler, a pair of scissors, crayons or markers, and a notebook or journal.

1. Fold the piece of paper in half, then place the opened book on the crease in the center of the paper. Trace an outline around the book.

2. Remove the book and extend the outline you have drawn to the edges of the paper. The lines you have drawn are fold lines.

3. Fold along the top line and the bottom line, then fold in along the right-hand line. You now have a pocket flap on the right side of your book jacket.

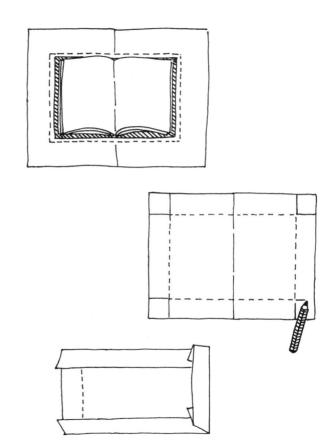

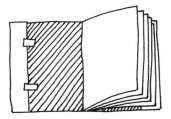

4. Slip the right side of your book's cover into this pocket flap. Tape the flap in place.

5. Fold the left side of the book jacket around the closed book. Crease the jacket along the book's left edge, then fold it sharply along the crease.

6. Slip the left side of your book cover into the pocket flap. Tape this flap in place.

7. Decorate your jacket with the stamps, leaving a blank space for your name or the name of your book.

49

DROP PATTERNS

Until now, most of the patterns shown in this book were created by placing motifs in rows that aligned side by side. Drop patterns create a very different effect. An easy way to experiment with drop patterns is to print three identical vertical pattern bands. Cut them out and place them side by side. Move the center band up and down to see how dropping a row of motifs changes the pattern.

Rows of tiles make large beautiful drop patterns. Try experimenting with cut-out rows of tiles.

The grid on page 59 will help you make small motif drop patterns. Use the grid as a guide under the paper you are printing on. Never print directly on the grid.

51

DIAMOND PATTERNS

Motifs look very different when they are placed on a diagonal axis. Can you find ten diagonal patterns in these two pattern pictures?

53

RADIAL PATTERNS

Radial patterns fan out from a central core. A daisy makes a radial pattern, and so does a snowflake. Many motifs can be used to create radial patterns. Some are easiest to stamp out without using a grid.

Other radial patterns are based on equilateral triangles. The grid on page 61 will help you stamp out radial patterns using these two motifs.

Here are some helpful shapes you can find within the radial grid.

LAYING OUT YOUR DESIGNS USING GRIDS

The easiest way to stamp out a neat and regular pattern is to use a grid. Four grids are included here. Place a piece of paper over the grid, then carefully stamp the motif or motifs you have chosen in the squares or triangles. Never stamp directly on the grids! Think of each row in the grid as a pattern band.

You can also make larger grid sheets than you find in this book using a ruler and a pencil or marker. When you are finished, make photocopies of the sheet to use for future projects.

The first grid is the simplest. The second creates drop patterns. The third is a grid for diamond patterns, and the fourth one can be used to create radial patterns with the two equilateral triangle stamps.

The diagrams on the opposite page illustrate how the thin lines on the grids can help you vary the spaces in your patterns

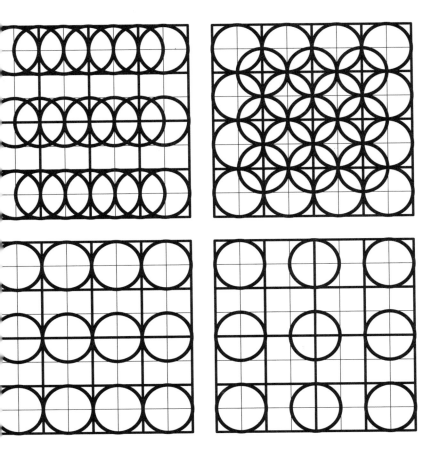

57

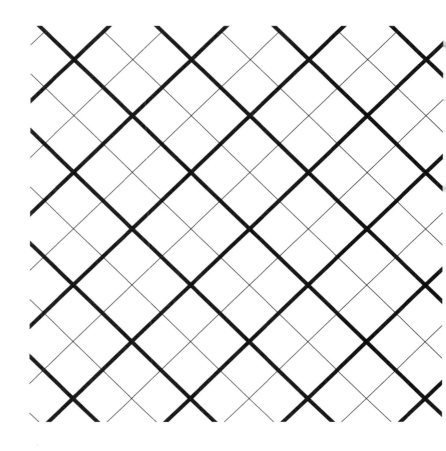

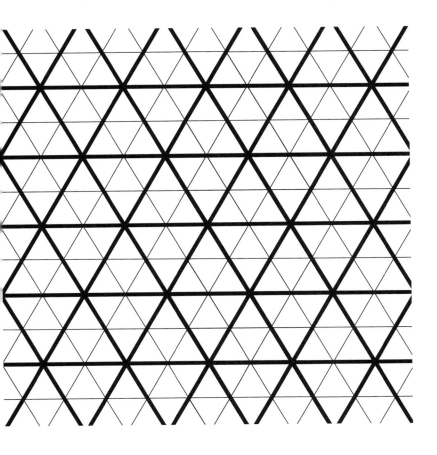

61

MAKE A VASE

You will need an empty, washed milk or juice carton, four sheets of paper, a pair of scissors, glue, and crayons, markers, or colored pencils.

1. To make a base, cut the carton to a height of four inches.

2. Using these motifs stamp out the pattern shown on the right on four sheets of paper.

3. After stamping out the pattern, close the semicircles in the top and bottom rows, turning them into small circles.

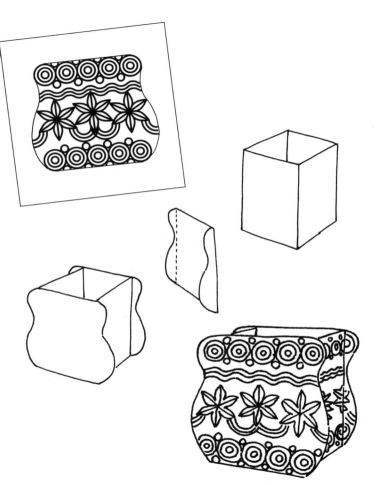

4. Now draw an outline around the edges of the patterns. Color your design. Next cut around the outlines.

5. Using glue or double-sided tape, attach the paper shapes to each side of the carton. Finally, glue, staple, or tape the edges of your vase together.

Put some flowers in the vase, or use it to store pencils or paperclips.

63

MAKE NOTE CARDS, STATIONERY, GIFT WRAP, AND MORE

Using the stamps in this kit, paper, and color, it's easy to make note cards, note paper, envelopes, postcards, invitations, wrapping pap placecards, and bookmarks—anything you can imagine! Your creations will be unique and much less expensive than stationery items you buy in stores.

You will need a selection of papers, a pair of scissors, a ruler, and tape, glue, or rubber cement. coloring your designs, you can work with markers, crayons, or pencils. When you want a thick layer of color or need to cover broad ar quickly, try using oil pastels, like Cray-Pas®. If you are working with board or heavy paper, poster paints are also suitable.

Colored ink pads, available at stationery stores, add variety to your designs. Gold and silver metallic markers add an elegant touch; they are perfect for holiday cards.

Plain white paper or board is fine for most of the things you will make, but it's fun to experiment with other surfaces. Many designs are attractiv stamped out on colored construction paper: Stamp out a pattern composed of leaves on green paper, one of flowers on rose paper, one stars on rich blue paper, and so forth. For small projects, brightly colore origami paper is handy. You can also glue a piece of colored paper to a piece of white paper. Fold the sheets in half, then stamp out a design o the colored paper. Write your message inside on the white paper.

ry stamping out a design on tissue paper, then color it with markers. The transparent color and translucent paper create a beautiful effect, rather like stained glass.

Because it comes in large sheets, tissue paper is excellent for making gift wrap. Newspaper is also a good choice. Use pages without too many headlines and with small type (the financial pages are perfect). After you've stamped out your design, color it with bold bright colors; the print makes an attractive background. Rolls of craft paper are also good for gift wrap. You can flatten a plain shopping bag, stamp out a pattern on it, then use it to enclose a gift. Or try decorating manila envelopes.

To create large sheets of gift wrap, stamp out one page of your design then have photocopies made of it. Tape the copies together, carefully lining up the patterns, and then decorate with color. You can also use a photocopy machine to enlarge or reduce your pattern.

Sometimes you may want to print only part of a stamp. For example, you may want to make a plain semicircle instead of a complete circle. Simply put a piece of scrap paper on the surface you are printing where you don't want the stamp to print. Ink the stamp, apply it, then remove the scrap of paper. The part of the motif you have masked will disappear when you remove the scrap of paper.

Here are five ways
to fold note cards.

This is a simple way to make an envelope. First fold the envelope paper around your card. Remove the card for later steps of folding, cutting, and fastening shut. Decorate the finished envelope as you wish.

You can transform ordinary paper and envelopes into your own personal stationery using the stamps.

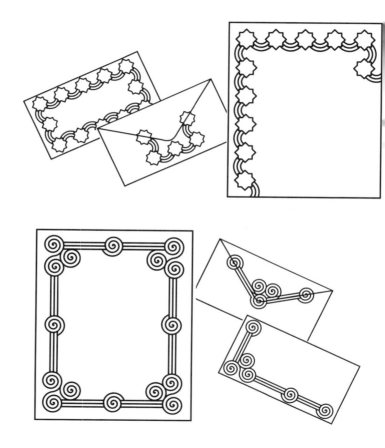

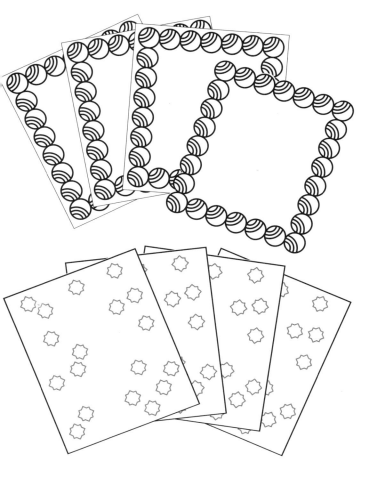

Use the circle stamp and the quarter-circle stamp to create this pattern. Cut around the design to make writing paper with a scalloped border.

Stamp this design in a light-colored or metallic ink, then write over the entire sheet you've just printed.

69

It's easy to make all kinds of note cards. When you are designing shaped cards, remember that one edge must remain uncut.

HOUSEWARMING

BEACH PARTY

COSTUME PARTY

GET WELL

GARDEN PARTY

CHRISTMAS CARD

Nothing is nicer than a personalized note. Borrow letters from this stamp alphabet or use the stamps to create your own alphabet. Then send special messages to a friend.

These designs are all great for gift wrap.

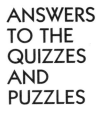

ANSWERS TO THE QUIZZES AND PUZZLES

PAGE 21

PAGE 26

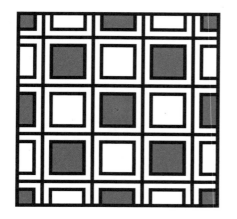

e dotted lines show where you will need to complete the pattern
th a pencil, crayon, or marker.

ISLAMIC PLATES

TOP

BOTTOM

MODEL OF A SERVANT

NECK-AMPHORA

Use the half circle stamp to make the concentric circles.

Use the quarter circle stamp to make this rope shape.

Cross this stamp over itself

to make this design.

EGYPTIAN PATTERNS

The dotted lines represent areas you should complete with a marker.

CRIB QUILT

PAGE 45

PERUVIAN TUNIC

The stamp overlaps in the two places marked by asterisks.

PAGE 46

MEDIEVAL PLAQUE AND ITALIAN ALBARELLO

The dotted lines represent areas you should complete.

PAGE 47

IRANIAN PRAYER NICHE

CREDITS

BOOK:

Page 5: Lamp, American, 1855–67,
Funds from various donors, 1967, 67.7.23.

Page 8: Mosaic, Roman, ca. A.D. 138–180,
Gift of Susan Dwight Bliss, 1945, 45.16.3.

Page 9 (top): Dish, Italian, ca. 1490–1500,
Fletcher Fund, 1946, 46.85.30.

Page 9 (bottom): Bull Holding a Vase, Proto-Elamite,
ca. 2900 B.C., Purchase, Joseph Pulitzer Bequest, 1966,
66.173.

Page 10 (top): Woman's theatrical jacket, Chinese,
19th century, Gift of Alan Priest, 1962, 62.27.2.

Page 10 (bottom): Ewer, Anatolian, ca. 2100 B.C.,
Harris Brisbane Dick Fund, 1957, 57.67.

Page 11: Red-figured Calyx-krater, Euphronios
(painter) and Euxitheos (potter), Greek, ca. 515 B.C.,
Purchase, Bequest of Joseph H. Durkee, Gift of Darius
Ogden Mills and Gift of C. Ruxton Love, by exchange,
1972, 1972.11.10.

Page 12: Study, Italian, ca. 1476–80,
Rogers Fund, 1939, 39.153.

Page 13 (top): Frog pendant, Precolumbian-
Panamanian, 12th–14th century, The Michael C.
Rockefeller Memorial Collection, Bequest of
Nelson A. Rockefeller, 1979, 1979.206.1072.

Page 13 (bottom): Commemorative head, Nigerian,
16th century, The Michael C. Rockefeller Memorial
Collection, Bequest of Nelson A. Rockefeller, 1979,
1979.206.86.

Page 14: Courtyard, Syrian, 1707, Gift of The Hagop
Kevorkian Fund, 1970, 1970.170.

Page 16 (top): Parade shield, French, ca. 1700,
Rogers Fund, 1904, 04.3.260.

Page 16 (bottom): Vessel in the form of a boar,
Southwest Iran, ca. 2900 B.C., Purchase,
Rogers Fund and Anonymous Gift, 1979, 1979.71.

Page 40 (top): Plate, Turkish, late 16th century,
Gift of W. B. Osgood Field, 1902, 02.5.55.

Page 40 (bottom): Bowl, Iraqi, 9th century,
Rogers Fund, 1952, 52.114.

Page 41: Offering Bearer, Egyptian (Thebes), ca. 200
B.C., Rogers Fund and Edward S. Harkness Gift, 1920,
20.3.7.

Page 42: Black-figured Neck-amphora, Greek, second
quarter of 7th century B.C., Rogers Fund, 1911,
11.210.1.

Page 43: Ceiling patterns (Tomb of Nebamun and
Ipuky), Egypt, ca. 1570–1320 B.C. (Dynasty 18),
Rogers Fund, 1930, 30.4.102.

Page 44: Crib Quilt, American, ca. 1840,
Friends of the American Wing Fund, 1989,
1989.255.

Page 45: Shirt, Peruvian, 7th–8th century,
Bequest of Jane Costello Goldberg, from the
collection of Arnold I. Goldberg, 1987, 1987.394.706

Page 46 (top): Plaque, German, 1150–1200, Gift of J
Pierpont Morgan, 1917, 17.190.437.

Page 46 (bottom): Albarello, Italian, ca. 1500,
Purchase, Fletcher Fund, 1946, 46.85.23.

Page 47: Niche, Iranian, ca. 1354, Harris Brisbane
Dick Fund, 1939, 39.20.